Miss Perilla Magilla
& her marvellous desk

Elowen Press
WWW.ELOWENPRESS.COM

Miss Perilla Magilla and Her Marvellous Desk

by C.L. Scott (@CLScottAuthor)

Copyright © 2022 C.L. Scott

Illustrations by Laura McKenzie Atkins (@Weebird20art)

All rights reserved. This book or any portion thereof may not be reproduced or used in any manner whatsoever without the express written permission of the publisher except for the use of brief quotations in a book review.

ISBN: 978-1-8384323-3-1

Funded via IndieGoGo by:

Aine Davis, Andrew & Cathy Goud, Bethan Lisles, Chris Irvine, Clare McGowan, David and Judith Poots, David Scott, Davina Darmanin, Day Morgan, Diane Henshel, Ellie & Steve Herron, Eloise Walden Pursell, Emily Kitchener, Frank & Sadie Scott, Gary McKay, Gordon & Sharon Scott, Gwen Thompson, Holly McDonagh, Ivor Wallace, John Fondse, Laura Atkins, Liz Keech, Louise Patterson, Lucy Ross, Michael Dickinson, Nicholas Dunn, Paula Rogers, Pete Belson, Richard Bell, Rosana Black, Rose Saarloos, Ruth Kolman, Samuel Poots, Sergey Kochergan, Sharon McKillop, Stephen Durbin, Theodore Cullen, Will & Elisabeth Norris

Words by C.L. Scott

Illustrations by Laura McKenzie Atkins (Weebird20art)

'For Lily and Evie. With all my love.'

Have you heard of a place called Implestiltzland?

A place where fantastical things are at hand?

With gadgets and doo-dads and goblins as well,

tricksters and beasties and stories to tell.

Come with me now, and we'll take a peek down,

and see what's going on in Implestiltztown.

The Implestiltz people are pixies of sorts, gentle and slight and all rather short.

Nimble and quick with their thin hands and feet, the most precise creatures you ever could meet.

They do delicate work with their delicate hands, clockwork and woodwork and pictures with sand.

But if you want something special, you must pay a call,

on Miss Perilla Magilla, the cleverest of all.

For Perilla Magilla has inventions galore,

not a day goes by where she doesn't make more.

Things for cooking and cleaning and fixing the car,

even a machine for counting the stars!

But however much colour they brought to the place they were certainly taking up far too much space.

She called on her cousin, Lobelia Blue, to come help her think about what she could do. Lobelia arrived at about twenty to ten,

"Perilla, you can't be inventing again!"

"I was patching the crack in the window sill," Perilla explained as she put down her drill.

"Besides, I've already thought of a plan, I just need you here to lend me a hand. I have an invention I'm willing to bet, will be considered my greatest one yet."

"Well where is it, this best of the best?"

"Right here!" said Perilla, unveiling a desk.

Lobelia was expecting something a bit... more.

"Just wait till you see what's down in the drawers."

Lobelia looked down and gasped in surprise,

inside the drawer was humongous in size!

"There's room for everything, and still more to spare!

I bet you could fit your whole house into there!"

So the ladies began to pack things away,

finding each object the best place to stay.

The lovely self-making four poster bed,

the cherry red, hill climbing, super speed sled.

A heavy contraption with brass pumps and vats,

for a hassle free way to bathe people's pet cats.

A twisty device with scissors and combs,

that could make lovely hair styles on the baldest of domes.

A detailed

scale model of

Saturn's third moon,

and a

strange little

sculpture made

completely of spoons.

A preserved prehistoric dinosaur nest,

and twenty-three all weather

colour change vests.

Snow globes with real snow, sunshine in a can,

and pencils with colours from scarlet to tan.

A hot air balloon, a big box of springs,

and several strange invisible things.

All of the books, and a bookcase as well,

and a winter time map of Blishamajel.

Then a bright purple carpet, now that was the worst,

for of course they should have brought that one down first!

Then lanterns and candles to light up the way,

and feathers arranged in a fetching display.

Nic-nacs and pictures, a whole jamboree,

and a big copper kettle for making the tea.

All the clutter and mess went into that drawer,

'til the girls were too tired to move anymore.

They flopped onto the couch to get their breath back, when they saw that the sky had nearly turned black.

Perilla nodded and let out a yawn.

"At least I'll get some sleep before dawn."

So Lobelia went home in her apple red car,

and Perilla sat back and looked up at the stars.

Her machine counted on, its lens fixed on the sky, and Perilla let out a long echoing sigh.

She looked round the room, at the bare floor and walls, and sighed again when she looked at the hall.

She got into bed and tucked herself in,

pulling the blankets right up to her chin.

She tossed and she turned but she just couldn't sleep,

not without her machines with their hummings and beeps.

She still tried to sleep, but the problem was clear,

so she rose with the shout...

IT'S TOO EMPTY IN HERE!

She dashed down the hall with her duvet in tow,

to the room where her marvellous desk had been stowed.

She climbed down the ladder and into the drawer,

tiptoeing carefully over the cluttered up floor.

She climbed in the four poster, duvet up to her nose,

and slept as soon as her eyes flickered closed.

Lulled to sleep by all the clickings and whirs,

a sound that was so completely hers.

CPSIA information can be obtained
at www.ICGtesting.com
Printed in the USA
LVRC091425140522
718478LV00008B/443